GHOST HOUSES

poems

EJ EVANS

Clare Songbirds Publishing House Poetry Series
ISBN 978-1-957221-00-7
Clare Songbirds Publishing House
Ghost Houses © 2021 EJ Evans

Printed in the United States of America
FIRST EDITION

140 Cottage Street
Auburn, New York 13021
www.claresongbirdspub.com

Contents

To Heidi Ravven

The Sleeper Agent

You have been placed by birth
in a strange country, among strange people,
where you are intended to play a crucial role
though no one yet knows what that will be.
Keep in mind the name you've been given
is an alias. Grow up, learn the local language,
learn everything you can, under cover
of the convenient identity provided for you.
There is no guarantee that your mission will succeed.
Mostly you must make connections--some will prove real
and some false--and persevere,
though admittedly you will have little to go on.
Expect many failures and dead ends.
Much later in life you may find clues
to your real identity and your real mission,
or perhaps not. Still it will have been enough
that you were always there, steadfastly faithful
to the mystery.

A Way

I am sending back a message
that becomes many messages

I am diffuse within winter rooms
the frames of the windows shape the light

the snow makes the streets fade away

when I go out I walk carefully

the house is full of shelves
the kitchen is cold in the mornings

the places I knew have faded back into the world

whatever I've learned has passed through me
when there has been sorrow I've tried to give it space

I am sending from my most recent self

Staying Home

When I first came here I saw
the house as a channel for the drift of time
the light breathing in and out
slowly through the windows
under the high ceilings
and the antique fixtures
the floorboards incised with age
within this arrangement
we dissolve into each night
and are reconstituted in the day
in a labyrinth of doors
and the rooms filled with books
in which we read each other
these our various ways of seeing
awake and content
to be among all these objects
left out in the open

Seventh Summer

I am sitting in a chair in a yellow room,
in a house in a village at the end of an orbit
swept around the sun these many times.
The memories, the many people I used to be,
cannot keep up and they fall away
but the house rings deep now with variations
of light and shadow and your nearness in this space.
Reading and sitting by open windows, waiting for breezes.
We drink iced tea, we watch the deer eating our garden--
late greenery, the edges of the leaves
already starting to change.
Somehow we have always been turning.

First Snow Coming

Every day a little less light, and in the mornings
and the evenings the air so sharp with cold.
The woods are mostly silent now
and the season is settling in, finding its place.
Any world that is to come must be born blind
from this one. From the detritus of autumn,
from smaller and smaller things. The gradual
dissolution of the sun. The whole valley intent
and poised like this for the long fade and return.
You and me plain and diffident. Here by the windows,
in the failing light. Listening, day by day
deeper into the quiet which is our song,
song of the fade and return.

Voyager

Some time ago my father emerged from old country,
from shadows of dim green hills extending far back.
He was strong but an outward-seeking thing pushed him
with a ruthless insistence, drove him west
and he came up against the coast. A busy beach town
under too-bright skies. And then another, and others.
So that his real home was a path, a movement among the places.
Even the warmest and brightest of them couldn't hold him.
And all along the way the sea was there for him, close enough
to hear the surf at night. In the later years the moves
became farther, as if on a widening spiral. Until finally
I found myself wading into the sea, carrying his ashes.
I poured them out and watched them drift down
through the water. And felt, even then, the momentum.

Sex

It's not that we are searching for something in each other,
but that something is searching, through these devious means,
for us. That the spirit powers must be real and present somewhere
we infer from this, all the ways in which they compel our devotions,
distantly perhaps but ever relentless as the tides. Even so,
we must fear deep down in the lonely dark that we are never
quite well or whole enough, nor ever quite ready,
for these the intenser graces. We start out with empty spaces in us
and they become larger, become deserts waiting for rain.
Over them the stars rise and fall, the day turns and bends toward night,
as the body turns and turns in its blindness, seeking some way,
any way, of seeing. Touch follows touch and a path is made thereby.
So we follow this wandering way, knowing no other direction,
closer it seems, to each other. Close enough perhaps
to hear a faint low voice inside one of us that calls "are you there?"
and in response the other that barely whispers into the dark
"are you there?"

Soaring

From the beginning
I occupied no particular ground or place.
The dark world was much the larger one.
The night air tasted of desert and distance,
of places where I did not belong.
Stranded somehow in a house, with a family,
indistinct, a house strange and lost
among other lost houses, in a stony valley
that I soared over in my dreams,
lit by a sliver of moon.
I did not know myself or where I came from,
or my home or my parents
or where they came from, but my night heart
already knew paths that led far up into the hills,
to where there was nothing but space.

Panama City

at night some welcome coolness like the mingling of distances

trying to discern what the underlying theme was

was it something about people passing through each other

or just the everyday breakage the turbulence

some leaves stripped from a camphor tree and flung into the fire

the risen light standing like a ghost of one's self central and alone

passing bottles and drinking in the circle of shimmering faces

under looming heads of palm trees and a sky of smeared stars

are we thus opened are we to be emptied

Living Alone

This is the last place. The house
is on the edge of the woods.
All the windows open and the wind
blowing through. There's the trail
that zigzags down the hillside
and farther down meets the meandering creek.
With damselflies and goldenrod.
With hawks crying out in the sky,
from their long high spirals.
Sharon said they are messengers of Spirit.
Every day I listen, listen. I hear them,
but I can never remember
what they have told me.

West Window

Down in the heart it is always autumn.
Always the row of pines
with their branches churning the wind,
and gusts full of leaves swirling past.
The clouds thinning out and the sky steel blue.
The light pouring down again across the lawn.
Late afternoons I watch it thicken and deepen.
You live there on the other hill.
When we are together
the long conversation continues.

Late Winter in the Valley

Every day brings more snow, and the snow brings
the quiet and calm. We have always been here,
always lived as shape-shifters. Always knew
the white meadows stitched with deer tracks
as places in the mind before our eyes saw them.
Knew the wavering tree tops as fellow supplicants.
I say we are not, have never been lost.
Every day the wind writes the snow into the land.
Something in us reads the signs
and so we follow, unafraid, in this house,
in this time, a way forward through the dark and cold.

The Sailor

He comes ashore in a morning of white and blue.
Everything he sees appears carved out of light.
He is in another city of another country
of another people of another language.
There are streetcars and shaded benches under trees.
The people he sees move within a world he'll never know.
In the late afternoon they play guitars
and drink wine at the sidewalk cafes.
He feels his growing separation from the passing time.
What is he searching for among the squares of the city
and the tree-lined promenades?
Night comes over the city and he wanders
the empty cobblestone alleys for hours.
He feels lighter. The stars drift through the sky.
He lets his feet find their own way.
He is content to be a city of one.

Far From Home

They seem almost like an old married couple,
there in the cabin at the edge of the lake.
They do not know yet that their love will fail.
Every day the lake is empty and silent,
the air saturated with light. In the mornings
they watch families of ducks swim
through the reflected mountains.
Sometimes the lovers paddle far out to the center
of the lake and then stop and let the canoe
drift in the wind. Sometimes they go walking
together in the mountains. They climb the steepest,
hardest paths. At the end there is always the sky.

North

I was still trying to break free of my life
that winter we drove 3 days north in a van towing a car
there was a space full of silence we held up between us
for the whole thousand miles
I saw at last that the world was fluid
composed of shapes and colors in motion
houses fences roads buildings and people
though there was a rigid core in each of us
surrounded by weariness
every place we passed was another small mystery
we could have pulled over and stayed
in any of the sad poor towns along the way
a father and son lost for years

1174 Dryden Road

On the day we moved in together we planted a red maple.
It was June and bright and we were open to the world.
Moving through the house, feeling its spaces,
I sensed everything already changing under the surface,
that we were but objects loose in our respective currents.
Later, on days when the sky turned dark gray
and the clouds leaned down,
to look out of the back window into the yard
and see the path the wind made through trees and tall grass
was to see my own life made visible. There were no fences.
At any time I could have let myself go,
could have walked out the back door, through the yard
and out into the woods, and kept walking.

How It is Here

The most important thing is that
every morning I stand in front of the big window

and pull open the curtains

and the sun is just above those two hills
the game farm with all those little fences

below Mount Pleasant
on its slopes the pastures with horses
barely visible from this distance

the fields dotted with foraging geese
sometimes crows

and sometimes they all rise
with a long undulating sweep into the air
and slide away through the sky like the ending of a song

and I am facing directly into the oncoming stream
that is the rest of my life
standing
as one rooted deep in the earth
and whatever comes will be mine

Three Years Later

The place where you live makes a center in the fields

the tiny lights of the house in the expanding dark

waves of dry grasses all around glowing cool white in the moonlight

the blurred dark shapes of deer standing away off in twos and threes

farther down the hill is the one crossroad

sometimes the headlights of a car pass by

I am far away but I am waiting for you to sing this to me

the whole world is a channel for this song

I am always listening please sing please sing it to me

Origin Story

The houses were small, the yards were small.
The cinderblock fences too close. A thin nearly bare tree
here and there. A car parked in every driveway.
In summer a hard glaring sky. In winter the streets full of rain.
People random among the days. Their movements were blurred.
Their speech full of echoes. All living unified under the wind.
Each night the starlit hills ranged around us
drew nearer in the mind. Their countless secret, empty places.
The future enormous, looming.

Slipping Away

What I remember most is that
I stumbled into love over and over,
though in different ways, each time
illuminated anew by the glow of discovery,
imagining myself the most fortunate of men.
But the world is on its own,
wayward, and of many devious currents,
and the accumulating past pushes us forward
into the dim future, separately
or together as chance would have it.
Those times when I tried so hard to hang on
to a lover who was slipping away,
which one of us was on the ice floe
and which was standing on solid shore?
Was it her or myself I was trying to save?

The Night Ship

By the time either of them spoke again
it was night, and the dark between them
was rarefied and calm,
with a few stray words floating in it:
"lost," "far," "forgotten."
He fell asleep imagining that a ship would come
that night, very late, from far away,
take a small part of his life and sail away with it.
And that this dark ship would come to him thus
every night, unseen, for the rest of his life.

January

All last night the rushing of the wind just beyond these walls
like a dark waterfall in my dreams.
Night and day and the house pushing back hard against the cold.
We would sit together before the fire but there is no fire.
We would share old stories but the stories have faded from us.
How unlikely we are. Rare as the glittering trees bowed in the yard.
And the white fields brimming over with light. Tell me we are living
in the place the world has made for us, is still making.
Wander through the house, drink tea all day, look to what is.
Let your heart be unfenced country, deep with snow.
Be of this timeless cold, its ruthlessness, its far-seeking.

Living by the Lake

When I was young I thought
some kind of sacred light
was in each one of us, but then years later
it seemed that we must be in it
instead. And now I have no idea.
The days break off and slide away.
I watch them drift to the horizon
on a layer of silence.
So little there is that sustains
or keeps us safe here.
The life I am still looking for
would be like birdsong
giving itself to empty air.
It would be an unrestrained
and anarchic generosity
circulating everywhere, mixing freely
within each separate day
with whatever weather there is.
In motion always, shapeless,
remembering nothing.

Going Out

Up early before light and out of the silent house
and dragging the boat through the dark
sliding the hull on grass down the hill
to the edge of black water and then in
working by feel standing knee deep
the water smooth and pure as ink
stepping the mast and pointing it into stars
rigging the mainsail and the sheet and pulling taut

a breath a pause to gain the moment
and then the pushoff aiming into dawn stillness
the smallest movements of the air are enough
slow glide with whispering ripples
holding the boom steady and close
all the wide water a single vehicle
for traversing the next instant

The Dream

The waking was so gradual, and the felt tidal pull so deep
it was as if I were stretched between two worlds
and for a long moment I could have gone either way
or maybe yet a third way, or more,
being for an interval paused in a directionless haze
in the center of a space,
so being momentarily uncertain
to which world I owed my loyalty and love
I could not choose but something chose me
and I came forth into this,
this one of how many possible lives, unsure
if I were rejoining a life I had already made or if
I had been claimed by something still larger.

Winter Solstice

After I was asked to leave I gathered up what I had
some crates of books my clothes a few pieces
of old furniture
I had a great weariness from the years of difficulty
and I gathered that up too
I did not know why I had all these things
I was patient and methodical
packing everything into my pickup
moving with mincing steps on the icy driveway
taking great care with the arrangement
strapping everything down to the truck bed
in the darkness and the cold
with snow flurries making random sparkles in the air
and I pulled the truck out onto the road and drove
toward some other place
the road a straight line running between snowy fields
under a hazy sliver of moon in the starless dark
I knew I was to take myself and what I could of my life
and cross over into deep winter
I knew that in time I would pass through
and emerge somewhere carrying much less
and changed in ways I could not yet know

Late Summer

You lay your life down as you go.
In fragments, and they are heavy
so you have to lay them down.
Sometimes you look back and wonder
what it is you have been making.
Eventually the work becomes lighter.
You find you can stand up straight.
You look around. You are on a terrace
overlooking a garden. The sun is getting low.
A row of trees makes a path to the sky.

Questioning the Body

The questions become more numerous and more insistent.
You want to know: why such limitations, such awkward constraints?
Your old friend and sometime adversary, with whom you contended
with clarity and vigor and pride, slowly grows into something different,
takes on obscurer aspects. Hints at a growing separation.
Its loyalties become suspect. After all this time to understand so little.
Was the body ever yours at all? Is it a vehicle for you
or are you a vehicle for it? Whose law does it recognize after all?
What is its native language? Is your real name
recorded somewhere in it? Will it fade into the sky or into the earth?
Is it fading even now? All along did it secretly belong
to earth's unseen places, to night deserts and storm winds?
Or was it simply a long coded message from the world to itself?
From a darkness to another darkness?

The Runaway Child

He was not brave. He could only run away in his mind.
Long ago looking out from his smallness
toward the farthest hills
he was seeking for a way out
that for him would be a way into his life.
Since then the passage of time has been
a long struggle to cross an expanse in himself,
yet it's still as if he has barely left home.
He is so quiet and small I often forget he is still part of me.
I sense his presence most when I first wake,
a plain man in an old house,
and look through his child-eyes
at the dawn light filling the windows,
the light that speaks to us always of distance,
and it's so quiet I imagine I hear him
whispering from within, his mantra,
just let me go a little bit farther.

Winds

Gathering new winds in the tall grasses
and the trees

unmapped and unknown in thought
or terms of marked or numbered time

this must be how life recognizes other life

all the way from the beginning
we have come

in the blooming turbulence
this long shared breath

Childhood

To live in yet another place
as an arrangement of rooms
the light pouring in making patterns

always the views of hazy hilltops
and sometimes far pale mountains

two figures, a father and a mother,
moving from room to room
speaking

years pass in the desert air
night messages and secret music on the radio

out beyond the fences
the schoolyard become vast under the white moon
no escaping this life

Turning With the Earth

I had become porous to the winter
in a dark time
a blurred human shape permeated with snow
icy stars and a shard of moon among ragged clouds

when spring came it was to be watched
alone
the thick blocks of silent light
the tiny flames of scattered flowers

each day dissipating into chill dusk and then gone

I followed the long drift of shadows through trees
I learned patience from the sun

floating in waves of the passing days

night air gone still and coyotes singing from it

morning and a fan of birds blown out into the sky
nothing between me and the distance

Florida Song

Even after everything failed
I found myself unaccountably still present.
In another wornout beach town.
Alone in my alien skin. Unready for the larger design.
I stopped looking close because the world was unraveling.
Into the heat and the wind. So many kinds of blue
to be lost in. Gradually people became visible to me;
they were all out of place. Superimposed awkwardly
on a flimsy disarrangement of things. I only wanted
to offer myself up. I did not want to know the soul's mechanisms.
Where we swam the water was clear and filled with light.
Sometimes there were jets going by, sometimes helicopters,
flying low over the beach, practicing for war.

The Music of What Happens

Roshi says impermanence, but I say transformation.
Quiet mornings flow into quiet evenings,
which continue into dreams, which become mornings.
I feel the past turning behind me, its great dark spiral,
funneling down to this. Bringing the energy.
Spring comes with its new colors, petals fluttering,
strange even to itself. Love is dissipated into the world,
again and again, flows into other forms.
The wind-bells ringing in the breeze, the empty table
on the terrace. Earth takes in the sun's warmth,
then offers it up as life, rich with possibility.
These steps I take, with such care, already changing
as I go. Becoming other, stranger steps.

DNA

Seeing some random streak of sorrow or rage
emerge in someone, friend or stranger,
reminds me of the dark current that has
always run silently below the surface of my life.
Through lovers, enemies, friends and family
this same current has flowed on,
our invisible shared nature. And before them,
through a wide web of ancestors
who struggled and died distant and unknown,
far back across continents and ages.
And further still, through ancient forests
that brought forth every kind of life:
creatures driven by blood, always seeking,
poised and wary, ready with teeth and claws.

Far Walking

I see now I spent my younger life
walking far up into surrounding hills
and back again. In passages along the way
I lived in a house, was a member
of a family. I was part of an old story:
I had been given energy—a little push
at the beginning—and space in which to move,
but no purpose or destination.
And the path I found myself on
turned out to be an ancient one.
Even time and the turning seasons follow it—
days passing like great, silent footsteps.

Noir

It was difficult at times, but after the wedding even more so.
Their house on the edge of town was like
a satellite orbiting the known world.
If I could be somewhere else, he thought, but there was nowhere else.
He sometimes felt subtle movements far away
as if a more real life were happening out there without him.
The summers were too long, the nights thick with heat.
They were passing through each other, darkly.
There were rages in the night, torrents of turbulent spirit,
there was an invisible lightning in her.
Each day there was a little less of them, a little more space.
He was tending toward some elemental essence he barely recognized.
Is this me?, he thought. When the breakup came
it was like a tree falling in the forest,
freely giving up its hold on the world, far from people.

The Accident

When we said our tense goodbyes in the kitchen
and I went out into the morning
it was into a strange purity
like a child's dream of winter a vision of wild gentleness
air thick with falling snow and silence
the yard new and unrecognizable the hard tangle of bushes
and vines newly made into soft and graceful forms
and the road a carpet of pure white stretching far down the hill
but on starting down my truck's brakes locked
and I was taken by gravity slow at first the truck sliding
and sliding all the way down gathering speed
taking on energy descending a smooth graceful arc
with me having become unexpectedly a passenger
all right so I'm being taken I thought strangely calm
I believe in the god of earth the final arbiter
who wields gravity moves all and treats all equally
so show me what you've got then
how far am I being taken how far does it go
not the first time I've tried to converse with nature
at the bottom of the hill the truck swung round
in a spiral and slid sideways into a ditch
dead-stopped in silence among trees
I climbed out into the same gentle snowfall
turned and walked the road back up the hill
toward the small warm house and the woman in it
and our small troubled life together
but paused halfway up and looked out across
the white fields and hills as far as I could
and even saw my own self seeing it all
standing there a tiny nondescript thing
but starkly alert breathing reaching out into the silence
to feel for the inevitable direction of my life

The Couple

Each has come this far traversing their long separate ways
each pulled through their own random stops and starts
along rigorous paths through different cities
alternating dark and light and driven
often by estrangements and by things broken
turning back and forth and turning away again
and learning to live with less and even to be less as they went
even at times to be racked and broken down to some primal
human elements but then to grow back as something changed

and having grown new strange scars showing
the imprint of the world of one's passage
and so having lived variously alienated even to themselves
have fallen together by chance to find these
cool clear days shared in high-ceilinged rooms
in the large house of many windows overlooking the park
in which to address each other with their plain common presence
no longer quite so sure of what is real
but resolute in their mutuality
still trying to tell each other all they have seen

Ghost Houses

The many people I've been have almost faded away,
but the houses I knew remain,
an obscure archipelago of islands in a life.
The first had white stucco walls
and a Studebaker in the driveway,
a short section of street in front,
and nothing else. And it led
somehow to the many later ones,
linked only by paths of airy memory,
each to the next in precarious succession.
Perhaps this has been my life, a scattering:
somehow I escaped each house
as it became empty,
seeking a kind of refuge in the next.
What is time to me now but this?
The houses all stand open in me, still,
enclosing nothing.
From here all the way back as far as I can see.
Each plain and rustic
in that permanent half-light.

The End of the Beach

It was my father's way to always tend toward warmth

when it became late for him a last summer grew up around him

in it he walked each single day alone

from his house down to the beach

he moved past the people and the piers and past the seabirds swooping

and the white buildings overlooking the harbor

he was whole then and he moved with calm in the roar of the light

toward the summer's invisible center

these are the places where he walked

he left footprints and his name written in the sand

The Outside

In the beginning of the beginning when you are small
you can see so much farther with your mind
there is but one world and it is outside
and it is trying to include you

this is not a choice the only direction is outward
in this way of seeing nothing is rough or broken
nothing is lost nothing fails nothing is of the caged self

Inheritance

There has been but one summer all my life,
to which I have been returned each year.
Because my father loved the promise
of the ocean and the sun,
at the beaches we paid our respects
to an elusive ideal of summer joy,
though underneath it all was an empty space,
and we rarely spoke.
California heat and blue ocean.
Swimming in the cold churning surf,
the waves almost too big for me, and then
lazing on the beach, hugging the warm sand,
eyes closed. I wondered then
to hear the crashing of the waves
filling that great darkness behind my eyes.
From the beginning of the earth
those waves had come, and they come still.
And all these many years later,
having gone to live north,
finding you there and being with you
among forested hills and valleys,
the most important thing
is that you always accepted:
this was how I was. You never questioned
why I had these waves in me.

Lake Mývatn

Autumnal days of windy rain and sleet,
of air with keen edges,
then finally a morning of stillness,
a chilly gold sunrise over the lake
and I no longer worry that I don't belong here.
The sky and the water and the stone
take the light equally and there is no center.
No next life of spirit, no world-to-come
but for these stark mountains
on which no one ever ventures but birds.
I brought my whole life of mistakes with me to this place
and now don't know where it has gone,
but the bare path that winds along this shore
gives a shape to my mind
for as long as I want to walk.

The Village

In the west over the icy lake the single star of evening
stands bold over the sunset like a beacon
and the network of narrow darkening roads
tangled among old trees fieldstone fences
faded houses that hold small spaces of warmth and light
and the tiny spots of human turbulence the subtle churning
of hidden lives with their minute motions gestures
invisible passions and sometimes quietly reaching out
past all walls into the deep world of frosty air
timeless their sporadic shambling shapes
dark-coated figures picking their steps in the snow
for how many generations
surrounded by these same looming trees this same sky

Though We Fade

We live along a spiral of seasons

a double helix because we are two

without fear and each in our own separate silence

with the faint sensation of descent—a gentle vertigo

we go wherever the house takes us

surrounded by birches and maples

turning, turning, toward nothing

most days contain little but space and light

we are made of particles that never rest

their tiny motions—a music for dusty rooms

though we fade someone may yet hear it

In Conversation

I'm here in my mind, you're there in your mind.
If we were to simply occupy this room,
sit in the fullness of the streaming light
and be plain and present in it
would we still have to figure what we think and feel
and find ways to say it? Or should whatever
is true and truly strange down in the wells within us
somehow rise into the light and
speak its love of its own accord?
This question will live as long as we do.
The main thing I want to say is that I have so much
that I cannot find ways to say. So much within myself
that I still wonder at, mostly disarray
and strangeness and shapes out of focus
and difficult to put names or handles to.
But I usually have trouble saying
even that. Perhaps it's like that for you as well.
As lovers of mystery, let us live by leaning,
each toward the other,
bringing our respective unseen worlds closer.
Feel how they gently pull at each other.

The Apartment

I'd hoped those walls might make a container for my life,
that I might finally take on a shape, however banal.
But the walls were permeable, as was my self.
After dark there were disturbances I wondered at;
they made random openings in the night:
odd fragments of sound, sparse voices, some hinting
of desperation. I tried to conjure their likenesses,
their secret stories, into my mind. I imagined
all my neighbors invisibly connected somehow
behind the scrim of dark, in the great space
of their common ambiguity. I began to wonder if I
belonged there too. If a kind of home could be made in it.

Jump

I still study dim grainy images in my mind
hunting through the thin shreds of the past
for the point in space and time of my beginning
was it that sunny day on a family outing
when I leaped off a dock at a marina
my small self momentarily suspended in air
before breaking through into a dark green world
and a glimpse of sun-shimmers on the surface above
with long rays hanging in wavering curtains of light
pointing down into darkness
my father must have jumped in to pull me out
though I don't remember that part
I don't know why I jumped
so many things I don't remember
but even after so long I still feel the falling
through that trajectory which has become my life
nothing underneath me but dark

Birds

I do not know what I was
when I first saw them or heard them clearly
being but an ambiguous earthbound thing
and at the end of my life they may be
the last thing I know
a final subtle distillation
of all my seeing and hearing
they have watched over me all my life
I have never learned their names
but their morning songs have brought me many dawns
when they glide on the wind they make of it a stillness
which I have tried so long to make my own

The Desert

Why did we go there
there was nothing but yucca and joshua trees

and the road straight through the stripped world
on which our car had stopped
and sat as if cast off from another planet

watching a tortoise cross the road
the only movement but for gusts of wind

all of us clinging to the surface of a life

The Soul on Its Own

Each day you rise to find yourself surrounded by empty time
and must cross again an expanse of hours and changing light
in which you will leave no trace

now in the midst of your bland movements
you sometimes pause and wait
for no reason other than to listen and to feel a stillness
freed from necessity

poor stray one in your wandering you have missed so much
where were the connections you might have had
all along did you expect that meanings would come to you

Learning to Draw

the first thing to learn is that every thing one does
even the smallest movement of pencil on paper
is a mistake

the teacher says draw what you see not what you think you see
but where is the difference
is it inside me or out

a room is an empty space filled completely with one's attention
and a few dustmotes drifting in the window's glare

the model changes poses and then changes again
each time the light wrapping around the body
with uncanny precision and grace

how far have I ventured out from my self in order to see

The Digression

It's not that we were defiant, it's just that at some point
we wandered or danced off the main stage
we'd shared with our stolid
and important forbears—still intoning
their long lines—and we kept going.

It's unlikely now we'll find our way back.
We're all this-way-or-that, walking on the grass,
becoming ever lighter as we go.
We watch clouds, we hold hands and sway
when the trees sway in the world's weather.
Eventually a random breeze may take us.

The Tarot

Surely you must feel when
you turn over the cards this time
you are another person than the one you were before,
that an invisible difference has quietly come into you
and pushed you a little further off the known track.

Turning face up one by one, the cards appear,
each carrying its lone primal sign,
like loose leaves whirled into your presence
by a wind from the outland
that is the world of your near-future self.
And each time you must learn to read anew
the ancient language of changes,
and to try to remember the question you had meant to ask.

House

The day runs on a little farther ahead of me,
carrying its long freight of wind and light.
The future is God, and all the things we see are flowing into it.
All will be forgiven, if only through forgetting.
In this story we are small and somewhere off to the side,
and the main things are the crusty dirt of these hills
and the whispering of dry grasses in the wind.
One must try to stay awake. To the gradual
thinning out of everything. Little is spoken here.
We think in birdsong. This awkward cabal.
This life we lead is rife with strange tangles.
The air is a delicacy. Charged through
with sporadic lightning. Here is our dinner in the quiet house.
Here is the rain starting to come through the open windows.
There is the road past the house,
mostly potholes now. It is connected to other roads,
and farther, to all possible roads.

Acknowledgments

Thank you to Ben Altman, Katherine Lucas Anderson, Peter Fortunato, Sarah Freligh, Mary Gilliland, Fran Markover, Fred Muratori, Heidi Ravven, Melissa Stephenson, Melissa Tuckey, and Diane Wiener.

Thank you to Clare Songbirds editor in chief Heidi Nightengale, book designer and director of publishing operations Laura Williams French, and the whole Clare Songbirds staff for making this book a reality, and for their kind attention throughout the publication process.

Thank you to the editors of the following publications in which some of these poems were previously published:

Aji: "Seventh Summer"
Confrontation: "Three Years Later"
From the Finger Lakes: A Poetry Anthology (Cayuga Lake Books): "Winter Solstice," "Late Summer"
Hamilton Stone Review: "The Apartment," "The Desert," "Slipping Away"
Hazmat Lit Review: "Far From Home"
Heron Tree: "The Runaway Child"
Iodine Poetry Journal: "January"
Main Street Rag: "The Soul on Its Own," "Birds"
Miller's Pond: "DNA"
Mudfish: "Living Alone," "West Window," "Though We Fade," "The Accident," "The Village"
New Mexico Poetry Review: "House"
Poetry East: "First Snow Coming," "Voyager," "Sex"
Presa: "Living by the Lake"
RHINO Poetry: "1174 Dryden Road"
Stone Canoe: "The Music of What Happens"
Woven Tale Press: "The Sleeper Agent"

Many of the poems in this book previously appeared in the chapbook *First Snow Coming* by E. J. Evans, published by Kattywompus Press. Thank you to editor Sammy Greenspan.

E. J. Evans is a poet and musician living in Cazenovia, New York. Born and raised in Los Angeles, he lived for many years in northwest Florida before relocating to central New York in 1995. His poetry and prose-poetry have been published widely in literary journals including *Poetry East, Confrontation, The Midwest Quarterly, New Mexico Poetry Review*, and *RHINO Poetry*. He is the author of the prose-poem collection *Conversations With the Horizon* (Box Turtle Press) and the chapbook *First Snow Coming* (Kattywompus Press).

CPSIA information can be obtained
at www.ICGtesting.com
Printed in the USA
LVHW031703041221
705286LV00004B/281

9 781957 221007